ENTER THE QUIET HEART

Creating a Loving Relationship With God

BY

SRI DAYA MATA

Self-Realization Fellowship
FOUNDED 1920
Paramahansa Yogananda

ABOUT THIS BOOK: *Enter the Quiet Heart* is a compilation of extracts from the talks and letters of Sri Daya Mata. The talks were given during informal gatherings in America and India at which she spoke on various aspects of the spiritual life. These have been published previously in *Self-Realization* magazine, and also in two anthologies, *Only Love* (1976), and *Finding the Joy Within You* (1990).

Authorized by the International Publications Council of
SELF-REALIZATION FELLOWSHIP
3880 San Rafael Avenue
Los Angeles, California 90065-3219

The Self-Realization Fellowship name and emblem (shown above) appear on all SRF books, recordings, and other publications, assuring the reader that a work originates with the society established by Paramahansa Yogananda and faithfully conveys his teachings.

Giving love to all, feeling the love of God, seeing His presence in everyone... that is the way to live in this world.

—Paramahansa Yogananda

Preface

Every human being yearns for love. From childhood, that was the tremendous desire of my heart; to me, there is no meaning to life without love. But I had the notion that I could never be content with imperfect love. The love that would satisfy me was a love unconditional, a love that would never disappoint me. My reason told me that in seeking perfect love, I must go to the Source; I must go to the One who alone is capable of giving such love. Thus began my search for God.

I was a girl of seventeen when, in 1931, my quest led to a meeting that forever changed my life. I had the good fortune to attend a series of lectures given in my hometown of Salt Lake City by a great man of God, Paramahansa Yogananda.* In the years that followed, I learned from him the way to total fulfillment of the lifelong yearning of my heart: perfect love, divine love — the all-consuming love experienced in communion with the Eternal Beloved of our souls.

During my travels all over the world, so many people have asked me, "How can I find greater meaning in my life? Is there an answer to the emptiness, the unexpressed longing, I feel within my heart? Where is the love I am missing?"

This, in essence, is what I tell them.

* See page 122, "About Paramahansa Yogananda."

ENTER THE QUIET HEART

*W*hat tremendous love, what soothing peace, what intoxicating joy are waiting for you in the calm depths of your being! That is where the Divine is to be found.

When we call to God from the quiet center of the heart — with simple, sincere yearning to know Him and feel His love — unfailingly we draw His response. That sweet presence of the Divine Beloved becomes our supreme Reality. It brings complete fulfillment. It transforms our lives.

God is a haven of peace, love, rest, and understanding from which we may gather the strength we need to cope with the endless demands of life.

Within each one of us is a temple of stillness that permits no intrusion of the world's turmoil. Whatever may be going on around us, when we enter that sanctuary of silence in our souls, we feel God's blessed presence and receive His peace and strength.

Let your mind rest constantly, or as often as possible, in the thought of God. In that thought we draw the strength, the wisdom, the great love for which our souls hunger. Be mentally anchored in that which alone is changeless in this changing world: God.

If we scan our inner self, we will find a hunger, a yearning, a need, for a kind of love that will consume us with total fulfillment; and for a complete security that nothing in this world can give—neither money nor health, nor any amount of intellectual understanding.

In God lies the security and supreme fulfillment you crave. Nothing on earth can equal the joy of the sweet, pure, loving relationship between the soul and its beloved God.

The whole world may disappoint us or forsake us, but if we have established a sweet and tender inner relationship with God, we shall never feel alone or forsaken. There is always that Someone by our side—a true Friend, a true Love, a true Mother or Father. In whatever aspect you conceive of the Divine, God is that to you.

When you go to Him first, how sweetly He fills your life and soul. Now when I look within and ask myself, is there anything my soul craves, always the answer comes: There is nothing I lack; my soul is fulfilled in my beloved God.

God alone can fulfill our deepest needs....

Once a person grasps this, he will look for a way to approach God. The practice I have followed is simply, first of all, yearning for God; and then cultivating a personal relationship with Him through devotion.

To have an intimate relationship with God, you have to get to know Him. If you were asked to love someone you didn't know, you would find it very difficult to do so—even if told of that individual's wonderful qualities. But if you were to meet that person and spend some time with him, you would begin to know him, then to like him, and then to love him. That is the course to follow in developing love for God.

The question is, *how* to get to know Him? That is where meditation comes in. All scriptures encourage the individual who is seeking God, who wants to know Him, to sit quietly to commune with Him.

In our teaching, we practice meditation techniques as well as chanting and prayer to achieve this. Some method is essential. You cannot know Him by reading a book about divine joy or love. Though spiritual writings do inspire fervor and faith, they do not give the end result. Nor does merely listening to a lecture about God. You must sit quietly in deep meditation, if even for just a few moments each day, taking the mind away from all else and focusing it on God alone. Thereby you gradually come to know Him; and knowing Him, you cannot help but love Him.

Keep an uncluttered place within your soul where daily you can go to be quietly with Him.

Throughout the day we have countless opportunities to take our minds within even if it is only for an instant, and talk to God.

If for even ten minutes a day you were to talk deeply with God, to the exclusion of any other thought except Him, you would see a tremendous change in your life. There is no doubt about it.

It is not necessarily long prayers to the Divine that touch His heart. Just one thought expressed repeatedly from the depth of the soul brings tremendous response from God.

I don't even like to use the word *prayer,* which seems to suggest a formal, one-sided appeal to God. To me, conversation with God, talking to Him as to a near and dear friend, is a more natural, personal, and effective form of prayer.

What is the easiest way to win anyone?
Not through reason; through love. So the
logical way to win the Divine Friend is to
love Him.

To your child, to your wife or husband or parents, you easily say, "I love you." And you don't feel embarrassed by it. Likewise, it is so simple to go within, to close the doors of that little chapel in the heart and say: "I love You, God."

Devotion is the simplest way to attract the attention of God.

When individuals come to me and say, "I don't know how to love God; I don't know how to talk to Him," I tell them, "Just as you are talking to me, just as you are pouring out your heart to me now, get into the habit of doing that with God." It is amazing how God responds to the simple sincerity of this kind of a relationship with Him.

Sincerity is the very foundation of the soul's relationship with God. It means to be able to go to God and talk to Him openly and intimately, in the simplest language of your heart: "Help me, Lord."

We ought not to cloak ourselves in false piety when we pray. This does not impress God. He is interested in what flows spontaneously from our hearts.

For me, the easiest way to receive response from God is to call to Him inwardly with all my heart, "My Love, my Love." You must go on saying it, even if at first you do not feel it. One day you really will mean it. "My God, my God; my Lord, my Lord. 'Tis all You, You." Nothing else needs to be said.

Practice the techniques of meditation until you become calm and centered within. Then take one thought and go on repeating it again and again and again, to the exclusion of every other thought: "I love You, Lord. I want You; only You, only You, only You, my God." Oh! how sweet it is to talk to God like that in the language of your heart. You discover what real love is. You discover what real joy is.

The devotee comes to that state, during and at the close of meditation, wherein his thoughts are expressed in a very simple way....There is just this sincere expression from the heart, the mind, and the soul: "I have nothing to ask, Lord. I have nothing to demand. I have nothing to say but 'I love You.' And I want naught but to enjoy this love, to treasure it, to clasp it close to my soul, and to drink of it always. There is nothing in the world—no power of the mind, no craving of the senses— that draws my thought away from this avowal of my love for You."

The habit of inwardly talking to God and loving Him should be cultivated not only by those who live in monasteries, but also by those who live in the world. It can be done. It just takes a little bit of effort. All the habits you have developed up to now are actions you performed regularly, either physically or mentally, until they became second nature to you. But you had to start sometime to create those habits. Now is the time to initiate those kinds of actions and thoughts that develop the habit of silently conversing with God.

Simply tell God in your own words — quietly, unheard by any other — that you love Him. Tell Him when you are sitting in silent meditation. Tell Him when you are on the busy street or at your desk: "I love You, God. I love You, my Lord." Let this be your last thought at night before you go to sleep. Try it tonight. It is so beautiful, the greatest joy. As you are falling asleep, as your soul begins to enter the state of restfulness, let your mind softly, sweetly, quietly chant, "My Lord, my Lord, my Love, my Love, my God."

When you feel sad and when you feel happy; when your body is not well and when it is strong with vigor; when things go wrong and when things go right, during all these times let there be a silent, steady flow of one thought: "My God, I love You." And say it from the heart.

How much sweeter life becomes, how much more beautiful, when in the use of the senses I relate them back to God. I can look at souls and say, "My friends, I love them." I can look at the birds and the trees and say, "I love them." But I know, "It is You I love, my Lord. You have given me eyes with which to see beauty in everything and everyone You have created."

When I see people whose minds are troubled by so many problems — frustrations, unhappiness, disappointments — my heart aches for them. Why are human beings plagued by such experiences? For one reason: forgetfulness of the Divine whence they have come. If you once realize that the lack in your life is one, God, and then set about to remove that lack by striving to fill yourself with the consciousness of God in daily meditation, the time will come when you will be so complete, so utterly fulfilled, that nothing will be able to shake or disturb you.

Even at those times when the heart feels dry, keep trying to feel love for Him. It must become a way of life; not for just a few minutes or hours a day, and not for just a few years, but through all the moments of the rest of your days. Then you will find at the end of the trail that the Divine Beloved is there waiting for you.

Each day along the way can be a day of joy, cheerfulness, courage, strength, love, when you unceasingly commune with God in the language of your heart.

Most people give up because they have the notion that God is not responding; but He does make known His presence in His own time and in His own way. One of the problems is that we forget to listen! Listening is part of conversation with God. As the Bible says, "Be still, and know that I am God."

People come to me, here and abroad, and say, "How is it possible for you to sit motionless in meditation for so many hours? What do you do during those periods of stillness?" The yogis of ancient India developed the science of religion. They discovered that by certain scientific techniques it is possible to so still the mind that there is not a ripple of restless thought disturbing or distracting it. In that clear lake of consciousness, we behold within us the reflected image of the Divine.

The Divine is always there. It is not that He suddenly comes from some point out in space and draws near to us. He is always with us, but we don't know it because our minds are not with Him. We allow moods, emotional upheavals, oversensitive feelings, anger, and the mis-understanding that comes from these, to so ruffle and cloud our perception that we remain unaware of His presence.

The scriptures of the world say that we are made in God's image. If this is so, why don't we know that we are taintless and immortal, as He is? Why aren't we conscious of ourselves as embodiments of His spirit?…

Again, what does scripture say? "Be still, and know that I am God." "Pray without ceasing."…

By regular practice of yoga meditation with steady attention, the time will come when you suddenly say to yourself, "Oh! I am not this body, though I use it to communicate with this world; I am not this mind, with its emotions of anger, jealousy, hatred, greed, restlessness. I am that wonderful state of consciousness within. I am made in the divine image of God's bliss and love."

Devotees who live in the consciousness of God find that they are always centered in Him, that the mind is constantly revolving around some aspect of the Divine: my God, my Father, my Mother, my Child, my Friend, my Beloved, my Love, my Own.

Develop a more personal relationship with God by looking upon yourself as His child, or as His friend, or as His devotee. We should enjoy life with the consciousness that we are sharing our experiences with that Someone who is supremely kind, understanding, and loving.

Most people have no concept at all of what God is. To many, God is merely a name. Some think of Him as having a form; others believe Him to be formless. It is foolish to think that He must be either with or without form: He is both. God's nature is limitless: He is "all things to all men." Each devotee may rightfully cherish his own concept of God, whatever most appeals to him.

The important point is that the kind of thought in which you clothe the Infinite should be a concept that rouses devotion in you.

If the whole idea of a personal God is inconceivable to you, then throw out all form. Concentrate upon Infinite Bliss, Infinite Intelligence, Omnipresent Consciousness, if such is more plausible to you.

Someone came to me and said, "I find it impossible to think of God as Father. I can't follow a religion that stresses the importance of loving and praying to God as Father."

I said, "Why be so upset over that? God is all things. What do you think He is?"

He replied, "I think of God as Mother."

So I told him, "Go after God as Mother. Think of the Infinite in that light. One day you will come to the realization that God is beyond all form, but that He also manifests through myriad forms."

To me, God is formless, infinite Love. Sometimes I think of that Love as my Beloved, sometimes as my Divine Mother, sometimes simply as Love. The formless concept is not hard to understand when you remember that you also are without form. As electricity is encased in a bulb, but the electricity is not the bulb, so you, the soul, are encased in a body-bulb, but you are not the body. When you see that God is all things, you can become divinely intoxicated just thinking about Him in any one of His aspects.

Think of God not as a word, or as a stranger, or as someone on high, waiting to judge and punish you. Think of Him as you would want to be thought of if you were God.

There is absolutely nothing we can ever do that will cause God to forsake us. He will never turn away from us.

We don't have to be perfect before God will love us. He loves us now, in spite of all our faults and weaknesses.

One of our great weaknesses is that we are afraid of God. We are afraid to recognize before Him the things that deeply trouble us in our souls, in our hearts, in our conscience. But that is wrong. The Divine Beloved is the first one you should go to with every problem you have.... Why? Because long before you even recognize your own weaknesses, God knows them. You are not telling Him anything new. Only there is a wonderful release for the soul when you can unburden yourself to God.

"My Lord, I dare to ask You any question. I never feel shy or embarrassed or blasphemous, because You are my Beloved. You know the simplicity of my soul. You understand my longings for understanding and wisdom. You see me with my good qualities, and with all the dark traits I have not yet been able to throw off. You don't punish me because of the flaws that have gathered around the purity of my soul; You help me. I do not try to hide my imperfections from You, my Lord. I come to You in humility, in devotion, in simplicity, in trust like a child, asking You to help me. And I will go on asking until You respond. I will never give up."

The Lord does not condemn us when we stumble, so we should not unduly berate ourselves. Instead, love God more. Be so in love with Him that your flaws cannot intimidate you, cannot stop you from running to Him.

God responds, not necessarily according to our merit, but according to the depth of our longing for Him.

Give to God just one thought of sincere love and longing and He responds: "My child, one silent call from the depths of your soul, and I am there in an instant."

In my relationship with God I like to think of that Divine One in the aspect of Mother. A father's love is often qualified by reason, and by the merit of the child. But the mother's love is unconditional; where her child is concerned, she is all love, compassion, and forgiveness.... We can approach the Mother aspect as a child, and claim Her love as our own, regardless of our merit.

The relationship with God as Mother is so sweet. A mother loves, forgives, and is loyal to her child, no matter what his errors. This is how God cherishes each soul. The Divine Mother is attentively concerned for our welfare and delights in our happiness. Who is more eager to be with the child, to give solace and joy, than the mother? Remember this truth when you are calling to God in the silent depths of meditation.

The ability to love purely and unconditionally comes from meditation, from being in love with God and silently conversing with Him in the language of your heart. I don't think there is a moment in my life that I am not talking to Him. I am not much concerned whether or not He talks to me. Perhaps I'm odd in thinking so. But I only know what joy comes from inwardly conversing with God, and then suddenly feeling a great thrill of divine love or bliss or wisdom pouring through my consciousness. Then I know: "Ah, Divine Mother, it is You who give that which I seek in this life."

When any good comes to you, share it first with God. When any adversity comes, give it to God and ask His help. When you don't understand something, take it to God; talk it over with Him and pray for guidance and right understanding. In other words, relate to God everything in your life.

In every human heart there is an emptiness only God can fill. Make it your priority to find God.

Remember Him. He loves you so much.

Learn to love God deeply. If you don't know how, then ceaselessly pray: "God, teach me to love You....Give me love. I stand before You with all my frustrations, anguish, sorrows, and disappointments, longing for understanding....Teach me what love is." The time comes when the mind is so completely at rest in God's blissful presence within that just taking His name once brings that love.

We must be sincere with God. What is the use of saying, "Lord, I love You," if the mind is away on something else? But take the name of God and say it just once with pure love, or over and over chant it with ever deeper yearning and concentration, and it will change your life.

If while I am speaking to one of you I am looking around at everyone else in the room, or at the clock, or at what is happening outside, you will think, "What is this? Her words are addressed to me, but her attention is elsewhere! She is not interested in me." That is how we make the Divine feel by our inattention.

God is as close to you as your thought
allows Him to be.

If we have faith that God is just a thought away, and ever lovingly attentive to us, how much more frequently we would turn to Him and rejoice in His company.

How we run to Him when some disaster comes into our lives! Don't wait for that. A silent call from the heart to the Divine will bring His sweet response.

If every one of you, from this day forward, were to get in the habit of practicing that silent communion and conversation with God, faithfully waiting and listening, you would see how He answers the call of your heart. It cannot be otherwise. He responds even in the midst of activities.

Be more cognizant of that inner world, where you can walk with God and talk with God, and hear His silent assurance that you are His own. This blissful relationship with God cannot come in any other way than by learning to reside more within, in the "interior castle" of which Saint Teresa spoke.

When your yearning for God is sincere and wholehearted, the moment you go within and silently utter the name of the Divine Beloved, your heart overflows with joy and love. This is what all of us want. No words can describe this joy, this overwhelming love. I understand how easy it is for saints to spend a whole lifetime observing a vow of silence, because there is so much blissful conversation within between God and His true devotees. Saints prefer not to speak much, lest the exploding bombshells of their words drown out the sweet voice of God within.

God gave each of us a quiet temple within, where no one else can enter. There we can be with God. We don't need to talk much about it. And it doesn't take us away from our loved ones, but rather sweetens, strengthens, and makes more permanent all our relationships.

When we go direct to the Source whence all loves come—the love of parent for child, child for parent, husband for wife, wife for husband, and friend for friend—we drink from a fountain that satisfies beyond all imagination.

Commune deeply with this God of endless love, who awaits you always in the temple of meditation.

Remember always: God is dealing directly with what is in your heart.

God has given us freedom of thought and privacy in the sanctum of our minds. No one can intrude upon that freedom and privacy. Therein, He has given to each of us the unbounded opportunity to express love for Him and to commune with Him. No one need know of our silent worship within—a sweet and sacred exchange of love and joy.

Love is the one tribute we can give that is worthy of God.

God is attracted to the compassionate heart. He comes to that pure-sighted devotee who relates to Him as the One hidden within every form. Think of each person as none other than the Lord Himself, wearing a disguise to see how you will react.

Strive to feel as God does for each of His children. We can cultivate such kindness and caring if in our dealings with others we hold within our minds the silent prayer: "Lord, let me feel Your love for this soul."...

All beings respond to love. Saint Francis was so steeped in divine love that even God's timid and hostile creatures lost their fear and aggression in his presence. One who is a channel of divine love becomes spiritually magnetic, radiating a power that harmonizes discordancy.

In the Hindu scriptures it is written: "One should forgive, under any injury.... By forgiveness the universe is held together. Forgiveness is the might of the mighty; forgiveness is sacrifice; forgiveness is quiet of mind. Forgiveness and gentleness are the qualities of the Self-possessed. They represent eternal virtue."

Strive to live by this ideal, offering kindness and healing love to all. Then shall you feel God's all-embracing love flowing into your own heart.

Don't allow yourself to be too sensitive, constantly stirred up by the emotions and the demands of the body and by external conditions. Try to remain in the inner stillness of the soul. That is where your real home is.

For years I have had this inspiring quotation on my desk:

"Humility is perpetual quietness of heart. It is to have no trouble. It is never to be fretted, or vexed, or irritated, or sore, or disappointed.

"It is to expect nothing, to wonder at nothing that is done to me, to feel nothing done against me. It is to be at rest when nobody praises me, and when I am blamed and despised.

"It is to have a blessed home in myself, where I can go in and shut the door, and kneel to my Father in secret, and be at peace as in a deep sea of calmness, when all around and above is troubled."*

Such security and peace can be attained by keeping the mind fixed in God.

When we are filled with upsetting emotions, hurt feelings, and restless desires, do you know what is really wrong? At the root of these sufferings is the loneliness and inner emptiness that comes from not knowing God. Our souls remember the perfect love we once tasted in complete oneness with the Divine Beloved, and we are crying in the wilderness of this world to have that love again.

The peace and harmony so urgently sought by all cannot be had from material things or any outer experience; it is just not possible. Perhaps by watching a beautiful sunset or going to the mountains or seaside you might feel a temporary serenity. But even the most inspiring setting will not give you peace if you are inharmonious in your own being.

The secret of bringing harmony into the outer circumstances of your life is to establish an inner harmony with your soul and with God.

God created every human being in His image, a divine image that is within every one of us—the *atman,* or soul....When you contradict that nature, you become mean, nervous, irritable, discontented, a victim of low self-esteem and other psychological inharmonies. But when you have reestablished the divine link between your soul and God, you have truly learned how to live. You become aware of a great river of peace and love and bliss flowing through you constantly, fulfilling you forever.

"Lord, Thou art in me; I am in Thee." Let the mind dwell on this thought-affirmation....With continuous repetition feel the truth of what you are affirming: Feel that God's abundant life is flowing into you as strength, peace, guidance, joy—whatever may be your material, emotional, or spiritual need. Feel that the constricting walls of fear, limitation, weakness, and loneliness are melting away as your being expands into His omnipresent embrace.

Realize that we are not alone, that we never have been and never will be alone.

God has no favorites. He loves each one
of us as He loves His greatest saints.

It is said in the Hindu scriptures that just taking the name of God can give one salvation. When I first read this, I did not understand how it could be possible. But I learned that it *is* possible, when behind that mental prayer is all the hunger and longing of your soul: "My Lord, I love only You, I want only You, I crave only You."

Many seekers have said to me, "But I *have* been praying." The Christian may say, "I have said my prayers every day for twenty-three years"; the Muslim, "I have been faithful in performing *namaj* for twenty-three years"; and the Hindu, "I have been practicing *japa* or doing my *puja.*" But still each one complains, "I don't feel I've made any progress. My mind is so restless. I'm so nervous. Why is this?" It is because these practices have become mechanical. You cannot win the love of anyone by half-heartedness or mechanically spoken words of love. Love must come from the heart. That is what is so often lacking in spiritual practices.

The means of finding God are many, but basic to them all is the need for devotion. What is the foundation of all relationships between people, what draws them together, but love? What draws us to a child but love? What draws us to any individual but love? It is a tremendous force in this world. When you look attentively at a child and say, "I love you, my child," the little one believes you. But if the mother says, "I love you," while her attention is occupied elsewhere, the child says, "Ma, look at *me*. Say it to *me*." Do you not suppose the Divine feels the same way?

In the Bhagavad Gita the Lord says, "He who watcheth Me always, him do I watch. He never loses sight of Me, and I never lose sight of him." I pray that from this time on you will silently watch that Beloved One. He remembers us always; it is we who are forgetful.

Let us turn to that Beloved One with devotion; but beyond devotion, be able to say, "I love You, God. You are my own. I could love no one — not my child, my parents, my husband, my wife, or anyone — except that You have instilled in me this power to love. So above all, I love You. I love You, God."

Ø

The greatest joy you can ever know is in silently talking to the Divine in the language of the soul. His is a love that can never disappoint us; I speak from years of experience. That is why I urge you: Love God, love God, love God.

Be drunk with Him who is Love.

Learn to develop such a sweet relationship with God that every time you are disappointed, every time you find some frustration in your life, you realize that it comes from God to remind you not to forget Him.

How wonderful it is to have that kind of relationship with Divine Mother in which you feel She is never absent, even during times of trouble and stress. When you have cultivated that closeness, you can talk to Her about anything, and feel Her sweet response and assurance. It isn't that you approach Her with self-righteousness or an attitude of feeling mistreated; but like a child going to his mother, you can pull the hem of Her robe and say, "Look here, Divine Mother, what are You doing to me?"

Adversity comes not to destroy or punish us, but to help to rouse the invincibility within our souls....The painful ordeals we go through are but the shadow of God's hand, outstretched in blessing. The Lord is very anxious to get us out of this *maya,* this troublesome world of duality. Whatever difficulties He permits us to pass through are necessary to hasten our return to Him.

Like a child, talk to Him. If you do this every night, your life will become anchored in Him. You will become like a strong tree, which bends in the wind, but never breaks. A brittle tree cracks and falls in just a little gust of wind. The devotee of God learns to bend with life's experiences, without breaking. His roots are anchored deep in the Divine.

The simplest way to win the battle of life is to keep the thought of God foremost in our consciousness.

There are several keys that enable us to be extremely active and yet not lose our inner peace or balance. The first of these is to start each day with a period of meditation. People who do not meditate can never know what tremendous peace fills the consciousness when the mind goes deep within. You cannot think your way into that state of peace; it exists beyond the conscious mind and thought processes. That is why the yoga meditation techniques Paramahansa Yogananda taught us are so marvelous; the whole world should learn to use them. When you practice them correctly, you truly feel that you are swimming in an ocean of peace within. Begin your day by anchoring the mind in that inner tranquility.

While working, every now and then stop and ask yourself, "Where is my consciousness? Is my mind silently watching God within, or is it lost in these outer concerns?" If you meditate and then try during activity to keep the mind centered in the Divine, you automatically begin to express balance in your life. And you become a calmer human being—operating not from emotion but from a deeper state of inner quietude.

In the midst of intense activity, when half a dozen problems are demanding your attention simultaneously, it is a real challenge to be able suddenly to stop what you are doing and think, "My beloved God, are You still with me?" When your silent call to Him reveals His comforting presence, then you know you are progressing spiritually.

If you follow what I am suggesting, the time comes when your consciousness remains unbrokenly in the meditative state —always with God. The devotee eventually becomes like Brother Lawrence: Whether he was sweeping the floors or worshiping God before the altar, his mind was constantly engrossed in Him.[*] That is the state you want to come to; but it requires effort—it does not come by imagination. Eventually, you will find that even while you are doing your work, whenever you take your mind within for a moment,

---

[*] Brother Lawrence (1614–1691) was the author of the devotional classic, *The Practice of the Presence of God*.

you will feel an inner effervescent well of devotion, of joy, of wisdom. You will say, "Ah, He is with me!" This is the fruit of meditation that can be enjoyed at any time, in quiet communion or in the midst of activity.

Love is the only Reality; nothing else in life has any lasting attraction or interest for the soul. Many years ago, I said to Paramahansa Yogananda, "There is one thing I crave in life, and that is love; but I want to receive it from God."

His reply profoundly moved me: "Then I say this to you: Take that craving into meditation; meditate deeply, so deeply that your mind becomes filled with nothing but that desire for divine love, for God; and you will know Him who is Love."

Seek a secluded corner of your home where you can be alone. Whether you are heavy-hearted, or filled with cheer and peace of mind, sit quietly and commune with God in the language of your soul. If you persevere, you will definitely find His response; it cannot be otherwise. The more you talk with Him — not in stilted, parroted prayers, but personally relating to Him in the depths of your heart — the more you will see that in the most unexpected ways you begin to feel His response within. We *can* know God; we *can* commune with Him and feel His love in our lives.

No love can match the love of God.

Pray to Him in the language of your soul: "You are just behind my thoughts, just behind my heart, just behind my breath, just behind the love I receive from my loved ones. It is all You—only You." God alone is with us when we come into this world. It is He who directs our lives, if we will but let Him. And it is He alone who will be with us when we depart this world.

Deeply, deeply call on God. Talk to Him in the language of your heart. Unburden yourself. No matter what your faults, do not be afraid to go to Him. He knows what we are; nothing is hidden from Him. Remember that He is Love itself—so compassionate, so understanding. God knows how strong is the delusion He has put into this world. To help us escape it, He is urging us unceasingly, "Look to Me, look to Me. Give Me your love. Cling to Me!"

Never hold God at a distance. Never! He is the nearest of the near, the dearest of the dear, the closest of those who are close to us.

Our relationship with God becomes very simple and sweet when we strive to remember how close He is to us at every moment. If we seek miraculous demonstrations or phenomenal results in our quest for God, we may overlook the many ways in which He comes to us all the time.

"Rejoice evermore," the Scripture tells us. "Pray without ceasing. In every thing give thanks." When we gratefully acknowledge our Heavenly Father's loving-kindness, we deepen our attunement with Him. Appreciation opens the heart to the abundance of God's love in its many expressions.

During the day, whenever anyone does something to help you, see God's hand in the bestowal of that gift. When anyone says anything kind about you, hear the voice of God behind those words. When something good or beautiful graces your life, feel that it comes from God. Relate everything in your life back to God.

Acknowledge the good in each moment, in every experience, looking to the Giver with a grateful heart.

God responds to those who have the simple, loving, trustful nature of a child toward the mother — open and receptive.

When anxiety, tension, and restless impatience cloud your consciousness, you will be unable to behold God's presence within. There has to be a calm, quiet waiting. Rabindranath Tagore expressed it beautifully in these words:

Have you not heard His silent steps?
He comes, comes, ever comes.

The devotee has to abide in the inner stillness, with an attitude of devotional, worshipful waiting. Then he begins to perceive that Joy, that Love, that Divine Presence welling up within himself: "He comes, comes, ever comes."

As you persevere, resolving never to give up, you begin to see that there is a sweetness growing within you that surpasses everything you have ever dreamed of—a communion with the Divine that nothing can touch....When you have that relationship with God, you truly enjoy life.

If you love God, your mind is always centered in Him. You are resting on eternal truth instead of being tossed about by the constant uncertainties of mortal existence. You become immersed in the stillness of the depths of the ocean of His presence within, where no surface storms can unsettle you. Then you have no insecurities—no fear of loss or injury, nor even of death.

This is the whole purpose of life: Find God. Be in love with God.

About the Author

Sri Daya Mata (1914–2010), whose name means "Mother of Compassion," inspired people of all faiths and from all walks of life with her wisdom and great love of God, cultivated through her own practice of daily meditation and prayer for more than seventy-five years. One of the foremost disciples of Paramahansa Yogananda, she entered the monastic order he established at the age of seventeen. In 1955 she became one of the first women in modern history to be appointed head of a worldwide religious movement. As president of Self-Realization Fellowship, the spiritual and humanitarian society Paramahansa Yogananda founded in 1920 and which she led until her passing in 2010, Daya Mata made several global speaking tours, and two anthologies of her lectures and informal talks have been published: *Only Love: Living the Spiritual Life in a Changing World* and *Finding the Joy Within You: Personal Counsel for God-Centered Living.*

About Paramahansa Yogananda

Paramahansa Yogananda (1893–1952) is widely regarded as one of the preeminent spiritual figures of our time. Born in northern India, he came to the United States in 1920, where he taught India's ancient science of meditation and the art of balanced spiritual living for more than thirty years. Through his acclaimed life story, *Autobiography of a Yogi,* and his numerous other books, Paramahansa Yogananda has introduced millions of readers to the perennial wisdom of the East. Today his spiritual and humanitarian work is carried on by Self-Realization Fellowship, the international society he founded in 1920 to disseminate his teachings worldwide.

BOOKS BY PARAMAHANSA YOGANANDA

Available at bookstores or online at www.yogananda-srf.org

Autobiography of a Yogi

God Talks With Arjuna: *The Bhagavad Gita—A New Translation
and Commentary*

The Second Coming of Christ: *The Resurrection of the Christ Within
You—A revelatory commentary on the original teachings of Jesus*

In the Sanctuary of the Soul: *A Guide to Effective Prayer*

How You Can Talk With God

The Law of Success

Where There Is Light: *Insight and Inspiration
for Meeting Life's Challenges*

Man's Eternal Quest

The Divine Romance

Journey to Self-realization

Wine of the Mystic: *The Rubaiyat of Omar
Khayyam—A Spiritual Interpretation*

The Science of Religion

Metaphysical Meditations

Scientific Healing Affirmations

Whispers from Eternity

Sayings of Paramahansa Yogananda

Songs of the Soul

Cosmic Chants

*Self-Realization Fellowship
3880 San Rafael Avenue • Los Angeles, California 90065
Tel (323) 225-2471 • Fax (323) 225-5088
www.yogananda-srf.org*